+REAL% WORLD MATH=

TRACKING ANIMALS

by Paige Towler

Children's Press®
An imprint of Scholastic Inc.

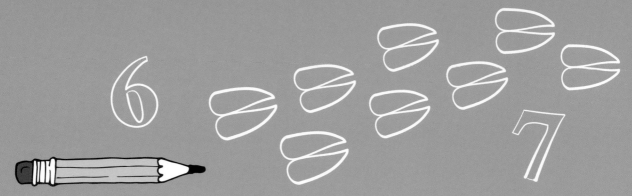

Library of Congress Cataloging-in-Publication Data

Names: Towler, Paige, author.

Title: Tracking animals / Paige Towler.

Description: First edition. | New York : Children's Press, an imprint of Scholastic Inc, 2021. | Series: Real world math | Includes index. | Audience: Ages 5-7. | Audience: Grades K-1. | Summary: "This book introduces young readers to math concepts around tracking animals" — Provided by publisher.

Identifiers: LCCN 2021000027 (print) | LCCN 2021000028 (ebook) | ISBN 9781338762037 (library binding) | ISBN 9781338762044 (paperback) | ISBN 9781338762051 (ebook)

Subjects: LCSH: Wildlife research—Technique—Juvenile literature. | Tracking and trailing—Juvenile literature.

Classification: LCC QL768 .T69 2021 (print) | LCC QL768 (ebook) | DDC 591.47/9—dc23

LC record available at https://lccn.loc.gov/2021000027

LC ebook record available at https://lccn.loc.gov/2021000028

10 9 8 7 6 5 4 3 2 1   22 23 24 25 26

Printed in Heshan, China 62

First edition, 2022

Series produced by WonderLab Group, LLC

Book design by Moduza Design

Photo editing by Annette Kiesow

Educational consulting by Leigh Hamilton

Copyediting by Vivian Suchman

Proofreading by Molly Reid

Indexing by Connie Binder

Photos ©: cover main: Photosimo/Dreamstime; 2-3 bottom: Jan Martin Will/Dreamstime; 5 top: Courtesy of Kira Cassidy; 5 center: Josh Metten; 6-7: John Platt/Dreamstime; 7 inset top: Hotshotsworldwide/Dreamstime; 7 inset bottom: Eric Gevaert/Dreamstime; 12: janetteasche/Getty Images; 13 top left: Andrey Gudkov/Dreamstime; 17: Rachael Hamm Plett; 22-23: Volodymyr Golubyev/123RF; 24: Natalia Pryanishnikova/Alamy Images; 28: Josh Metten; 29 top: Courtesy of Kira Cassidy; 29 bottom: Ronan Donovan; 31: Courtesy of Kira Cassidy.

All other photos © Shutterstock.

CONTENTS

LET'S GO!

1 paw print . . . 2 paw prints . . . 3!

What animal made these tracks? Where do they lead? Let's follow the paw prints and find out. Looking for animals so we can learn more about them is called *tracking*. So grab a backpack, binoculars, a compass, and your math skills!

Scientists use math to learn all kinds of information about animals. They can count animals to make sure groups are healthy. They can compare track sizes to identify animals. And scientists can measure how far an animal travels to find out where they live.

Today we are tracking animals around the world using math. Our first stop is somewhere very colorful. Are you ready?

wolf pack

Kira

MEET KIRA

We are joining scientist Kira Cassidy to track animals. She works in Yellowstone National Park, where she tracks the wolves that live there. Tracking wolves helps Kira see what they eat, where they live, how big their **packs** are, and more. This research helps scientists learn about how wolves live so they can protect these amazing animals.

Welcome to the Amazon rainforest!

This is the largest tropical rainforest in the world. Brown monkeys play high in the treetops. Green frogs hop from leaf to leaf. And spotted golden jaguars walk the forest floor.

tree frog

monkey

As we look at the colorful rainforest, let's think like a tracker and get ready to count. Counting is very important for animal trackers. It helps them learn if groups of animals are healthy. When there are lots of animals in an area, scientists know that they are doing well in their homes.

Lots of beautiful birds also call the rainforest home.
There are big birds and tiny birds. There are birds with bright yellow wings and birds with long red tails. Today let's count parrots.

1

2

3

4

YOU CAN DO IT!

Count each parrot you see in the photo below. How many parrots can you find?

Great job! You tracked animals by counting all the parrots. Now it is time to grab your sunglasses. Next we are going somewhere with a lot more sunshine.

A family of elephants marches through the dry grasses. On the African **savanna**, many animals gather in groups. Animals live in groups for different reasons. For some, like zebras, big groups help keep them safe. Others, like elephants, live in groups with their families—just like humans.

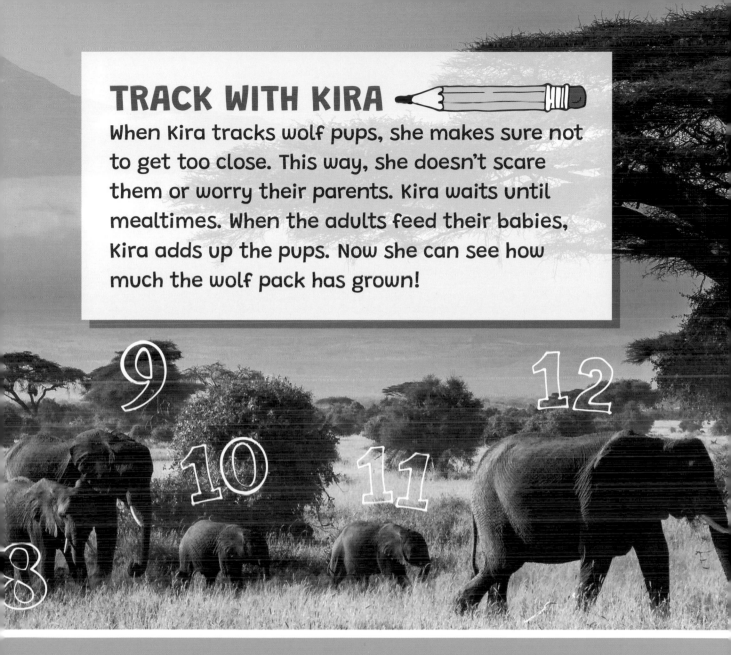

TRACK WITH KIRA

When Kira tracks wolf pups, she makes sure not to get too close. This way, she doesn't scare them or worry their parents. Kira waits until mealtimes. When the adults feed their babies, Kira adds up the pups. Now she can see how much the wolf pack has grown!

Animal families have moms, dads, aunts, uncles, grandparents, and more.

Let's get ready to use **addition**! By adding up the number of animals in a group, scientists can make sure the family is getting bigger and stronger.

+ = 🐾

Lions live in the savanna in groups called prides. A pride can have up to forty lions. These lion families eat, sleep, and hunt together. Here, one male lion has joined five female lions for a nap in the shade. Now there are six lions.

1+5=6

YOU CAN DO IT! ②

Before these three cubs were born, there were five lions in this pride. How many lions are in the pride now?

5 + 3 =

Yes! These cubs will be safe together with their pride. Now it is time for us to leave the heat. We are heading somewhere snowy, so bundle up!

20

10

 Antarctica is a large continent located at the South Pole. It is covered in ice and has some of the lowest temperatures on Earth. *Brrr!* We are going to need a warm jacket, gloves, and snow boots to track animals here.

There are lots of penguins in Antarctica.
Penguins live in very large groups called **colonies**. They
stay warm because they have **blubber** and thick layers
of feathers. They keep cozy by pressing up against
one another.

30 40 50 60

70

Even though it is cold, there are lots of animals that have different ways to keep warm. We can count these cozy creatures using the number 100.

80

It is a big number, but we can divide 100 into smaller groups to make it easier. Ten groups of ten is the same as 100.

90

emperor penguins

100!

YOU CAN DO IT! 3

Each group below contains ten penguins. How many groups are there? How many penguins are in this colony?

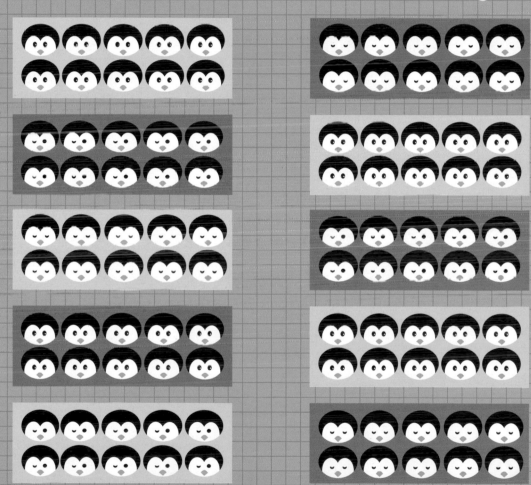

Hooray! You counted all the penguins in the colony. Now it is time to go somewhere warmer. The next stop has lots of animals and spiky plants that grow best in hot weather.

Dusty earth stretches for miles here in the Sonoran Desert. This **desert** is hot and dry. There is very little rain. But it is full of life, big and small. The saguaro cactus can grow as tall as a three-story building. Small scorpions scamper across the hot sand. Large bighorn sheep climb cliffs and mountains.

TRACK WITH KIRA

When tracking wolves, Kira looks at the paw prints they leave in the mud and snow. These are also called tracks. If there are lots of different tracks, how can Kira tell if a print belongs to a wolf? She compares sizes. Adult wolves leave paw prints that are about the same size as ones left by a very large dog. Kira knows that if the paw prints are bigger or smaller, they probably belong to a different animal.

scorpion

bighorn sheep

As we look at different animals in the desert, let's compare their sizes. Comparing

is a great way for scientists to track animals. They can compare different tracks to identify animals. Comparing the sizes of two animals can also help trackers learn more about them. It can help them tell how old an animal is, what it eats, and where it lives.

Lizards of all sizes run around the Sonoran Desert.

gecko

Many lizards, like geckos, are tiny. But Gila monsters can grow to be huge. From tip to tail, they can be as big as a skateboard! Their footprints are big, too. They are much larger than the prints left by a little gecko.

Gila monster

YOU CAN DO IT!

Let's track lizards. Here are two sets of lizard tracks. Which tracks are bigger? Which lizard takes smaller steps? Which set was made by the gecko and which was made by the Gila monster?

A

B

Following animal tracks in the hot desert is hard work. Take a deep breath and get ready to make a splash as we track another animal.

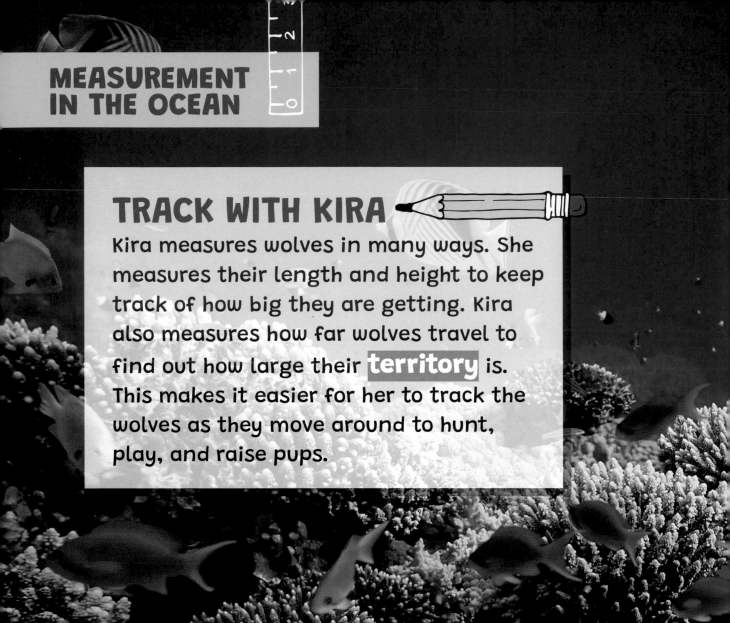

TRACK WITH KIRA

Kira measures wolves in many ways. She measures their length and height to keep track of how big they are getting. Kira also measures how far wolves travel to find out how large their **territory** is. This makes it easier for her to track the wolves as they move around to hunt, play, and raise pups.

The huge, blue ocean is full of life.

The ocean's water covers more of Earth than all its land put together. The ocean is also very, very deep. Down deep, it is cold and dark. Not many animals live there. Most live up near the surface, where it is warm from the sun.

A good way to track animals in the ocean is using **measurement**. When we measure something, we find out its height, length, or weight. Or we can measure the distance between two things. Measuring can show trackers how far an animal has traveled, how big an animal is, or how deep in the ocean an animal lives.

20 FT

**These dolphins
are diving deep**
to hunt for food. We can
use measurement to find
out which dolphin dove the
deepest! One dove twenty
feet under the surface to
catch a fish. But the other
dolphin dove thirty feet.
The larger the number, the
deeper the dolphin dove.

30 FT

YOU CAN DO IT! 5

Let's use measurement to track animals. Dolphin A is twenty-five feet below the surface. Dolphin B is ten feet below Dolphin A. Which dolphin is deeper? How deep did Dolphin B dive?

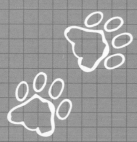

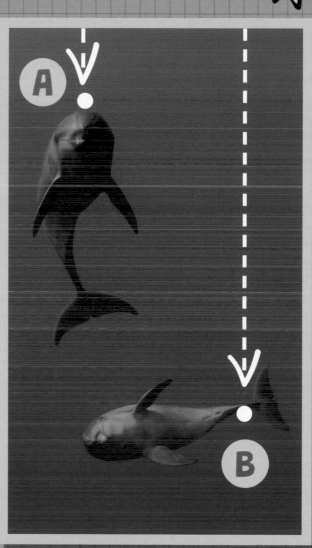

Wow—great job measuring! These dolphins are probably sleepy after a long day of diving to find food. And we have had a long trip of tracking animals.

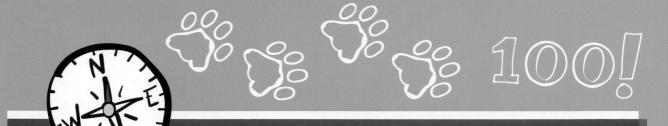

WAY TO GO!

Nice work tracking animals!

We followed clues to track big and small animals, colorful animals, and animal babies. We tracked animals in hot, cold, dry, and wet places.

We also learned how to track animals using math! We used counting, addition, the number 100, comparisons, and measurement. These math skills help scientists learn about animals. Math is so important every day in so many ways. You might be surprised how often you use it!

YOU CAN DO IT! 6

How many animals did we track on the trip? Which animal in this book is the biggest? Which one lives in the coldest place?

KIRA TRACKS ANIMALS

Kira Cassidy works as a scientist in Wyoming, United States. There, she studies and helps protect gray wolves as part of the Yellowstone Wolf Project. Tracking is a big part of her job.

Kira works with other scientists to make sure the wolves are healthy. To do this, Kira gets out her camera and binoculars. Sometimes she also grabs a heavy coat and snowshoes! Kira follows wolves to see what they eat, how they behave, and where they go. This information helps her learn more about them. She counts how many wolves are in the park. She measures paw prints to see how big the wolves are growing. She adds up the members of a pack. And those are just some of the math skills Kira uses every day!

wolf print (top); Kira's hand (bottom)

Kira also has lots of cool gear to help track animals. Some wolves wear radio collars, which send signals to computers back at the lab. These signals show an animal's location on a map. This helps researchers measure how far the wolves travel!

Tracking animals lets Kira and the other researchers learn more about wolves. The more scientists and the entire world know about wolves, the more they are able to understand and protect them. Thanks to math, Kira and her team are learning lots about these amazing animals!

Kira tracks wolves.

GLOSSARY

penguin

addition (uh-DISH-uhn): the combining of two or more numbers to come up with a sum

Antarctica (ant-AHRK-ti-kuh): the continent around the South Pole

blubber (BLUH-bur): the layer of fat under the skin of some penguins and other large marine animals

colony (KAH-luh-nee): a large group of animals that live together

desert (DEZ-urt): a dry area where hardly any plants grow because there is so little rain

measurement (ME-zhur-muhnt): the size, weight, or amount of something

pack (pak): a group of similar animals, people, or things, such as a wolf pack

pride (pride): a group of lions

rainforest (RAYN-for-ist): a dense, tropical forest where a lot of rain falls for much of the year

savanna (suh-VAN-uh): a flat, grassy plain with few or no trees

scientist (SYE-uhn-tist): a person who is trained and works in science

territory (TER-i-tor-ee): the area where an animal lives and defends as its home

wolf pack

YOU CAN DO IT! ANSWER KEY

1 **PAGE 9** 9 parrots

2 **PAGE 13** 8 lions

3 **PAGE 17** There are ten groups. There are 100 penguins.

4 **PAGE 21** Set B has bigger tracks. Set A takes smaller steps. Set A is the gecko, and Set B is the Gila monster.

5 **PAGE 25** Dolphin B is deeper and dove thirty-five feet.

6 **PAGE 27** We tracked five types of animals on our trip: parrots, lions, penguins, lizards, and dolphins. The biggest animal in this book is the elephant. The penguins live in the coldest place.

INDEX

Page numbers in **bold** indicate illustrations.

ABOUT THE AUTHOR

Paige Towler is a children's book author and editor. Formerly an editor for National Geographic Kids Books, she currently writes and edits for Smithsonian Licensed Publishing, National Geographic Books, Scholastic, and more. Her books include *Yoga Animals* and *Girls Can!*